Gus & Me

THE STORY OF MY GRANDDAD AND MY FIRST GUITAR

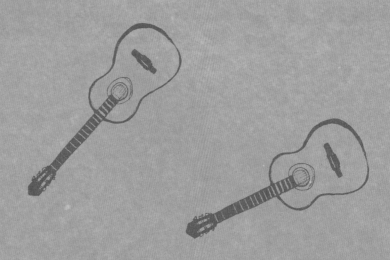

For Marlon, Angela, Theodora, Alexandra, Ella, Orson, Ida, Ava, and Otto

—KR

To my family

—TR

First published in Great Britain in 2014 by Orion Children's Books • This paperback edition was first published in Great Britain in 2015 by Orion Children's Books a division of Hachette Children's Group • Published by Hodder & Stoughton • Orion House 5 Upper St Martin's Lane London WC2H 9EA • An Hachette UK Company • 1 3 5 7 9 10 8 6 4 2 • Copyright © 2014 by Mindless Records, LLC • Cover art by Theodora Richards • Back cover photograph by Jane Rose • Cover design by Gail Doobinin • Cover copyright © 2014 Hachette Book Group, Inc. • The rights of the author and illustrator of this work have been asserted. • All rights reserved. No part of this publication may be reproduced, stored in a retrieval system, or transmitted, in any form or by any means, electronic, mechanical, photocopying, recording or otherwise, without the prior permission of Orion Children's Books. • The manufacturing processes conform to the environmental regulations of the country of origin. • A catalogue record for this book is available from the British Library. • ISBN 978 1 4440 1542 3 • Printed and bound in China • www.orionchildrensbooks.co.uk

Gus & Me

THE STORY OF
MY GRANDDAD
AND
MY FIRST GUITAR

KEITH RICHARDS

with Barnaby Harris and Bill Shapiro

Art by THEODORA RICHARDS

Orion
Children's Books

Theodore Augustus Dupree
lived with seven daughters near the Seven Sisters Road,
in a house that was filled with instruments and cake.

Theodore Augustus Dupree
could play the piano and scrape the violin,
blow the saxophone and strum the guitar.
He had been a soldier, a baker,
and the leader of a dance band.

SOLDIER

Baker

Leader of a Dance Band

But now Theodore Augustus Dupree was my granddad.

Now he was Gus.

There was nothing like visiting Gus.

The closer to his house I'd get,

the bigger my smile would grow.

By the time I landed on his doorstep,

I was all teeth.

He'd be waiting at the front door for me.

"*Fix the sink, Gus,*" my grandmother would call out.

"*Can't do, Emma,*" Gus would call back.

"*Keith and I are going for a walk.*"

He'd wink at me and whistle for Mr. Thompson Wooft,

and our adventure would begin.

Battersea Bridge

BIG BEN

Lord Nelson

7 SISTERS ROAD

We'd walk for miles.
We'd walk through towns,
and we'd walk through the countryside...
and Gus, he would hum every step of the way.
He'd hum whole symphonies as we strolled
from one village to the next.
He'd hum funny little tunes
as we wandered skinny streets and smoky alleys,
marching songs as we tiptoed around foggy ponds
and explored silent forests.

With Gus, you had no idea where you'd end up.

One time he led me all the way to the top of Primrose Hill
to look at the night stars.
"Don't know if we can make it home tonight," Gus said.
So we slept under a tree on the top of the hill,
with the sky lights above us and the city lights below.

Once Gus walked us all the way to London

and into the workshop of a big store

that sold instruments.

"Let's just pop in here, I've got to pick up some strings."

Inside, it looked like a beehive.

Gus lifted me up and sat me on a shelf

so that I could see everything.

Violins hung from the ceiling by wires.

Horns clung to the walls.

Men in long brown coats

fixed broken instruments and built new ones.

I watched as they bent over cellos, trombones, and trumpets.

They dabbed at the drums with glue

and tapped at them with tiny hammers.

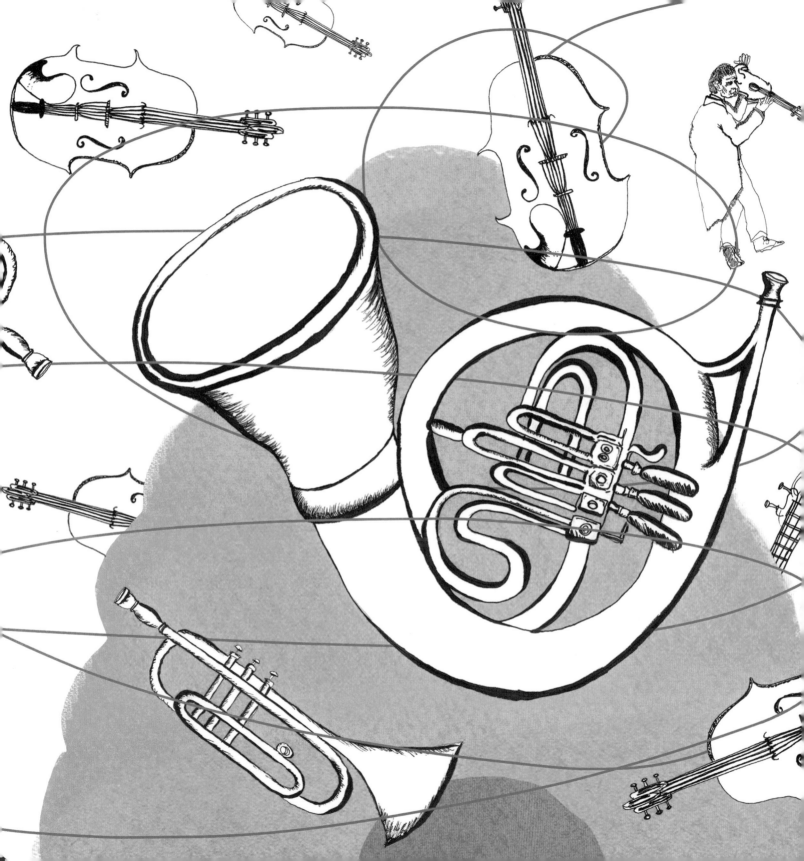

Men tested the guitar strings:
dinka-plink dinka-plink.
And the drums:
dok-dok fum-fum dok-fum.

DOK-DOK
FUM-FUM
DOK-FUM

My eyes followed a line of guitars
that snaked around the room on a conveyor belt.
And in the middle of everything,
big, bubbling buckets of glue went
blub blub blub.
It was magic.
I sat on that shelf, watching it all.

And right then, right there, I fell in love with instruments.

When Gus and I got back to his house that day,

I took a long look at that guitar

that always sat on top of his piano.

It seemed more beautiful than ever.

All I wanted was to make the strings go

dinka-plink-plink like the men in the store.

But I couldn't reach it.

"When you're tall enough, you can have a go," Gus said.

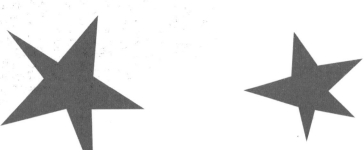

Every time I visited Gus, I reached for that guitar.
Even on my toes, I couldn't touch it.

One day, I felt like I was tall enough to grab it,
but I didn't even have to try.
Gus simply handed it to me.
"*All yours*," he said.

He sat with me,

taught me how to hold it,

strum it, and pluck a little.

"When you learn how to play 'Malagueña,'"

he told me, *"you can play anything."*

Dinka-plink dinka-plink dinka-plink.

And I practiced and I practiced on that beautiful guitar.

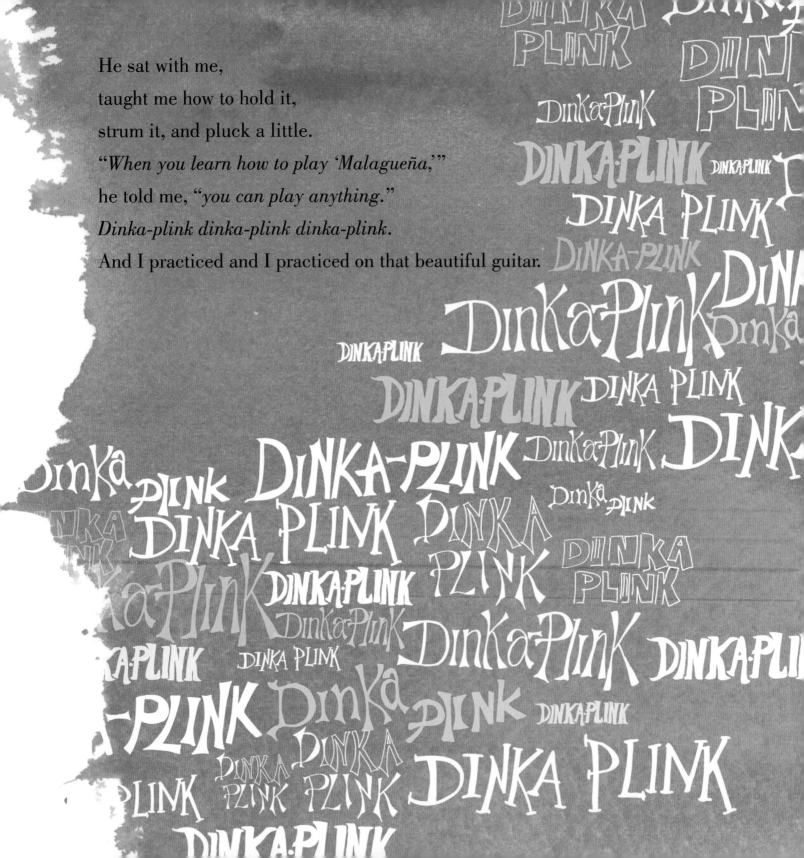

One day, Gus heard me playing
"Malagueña," and he nodded.
Then he said something I'll never forget:
"I think you're getting the hang of it."

After that,
I took that guitar everywhere.
I went to sleep with my arms
wrapped around it.

Even today, all these years later, I think of Gus.

Every time I walk onstage, every time I write a song,

every time I reach for a guitar and play

a few *dinka-plink*s for my own grandchildren,

I say to myself,

Thanks Granddad
Thanks Gus!

ABOUT KEITH RICHARDS

Keith Richards came from a musical family in Dartford, England: His mother, Doris, always had the radio on; his grandmother played the piano; he and his aunt Joanna harmonized to Everly Brothers songs together; and his granddad Theodore Augustus Dupree—Gus—played the violin, the saxophone, and the guitar.

Keith and Gus visiting in the 1960s

Keith, age 15

Keith grew up during and after World War II, when it could be hard to find the bright side of London. But Keith and his grandfather walked every inch of it together. On their walks, Gus took Keith to repair shops, and they watched as busy workers fixed broken instruments. One day, Gus showed Keith the major chords on the guitar and taught him to play the classic piece "Malagueña." This was Keith's introduction to music.

Theodore Augustus Dupree

Keith later began playing in a band with a group of friends, including Mick Jagger. They called themselves the Rolling Stones. Years later, the Rock and Roll Hall of Fame named them the World's Greatest Rock and Roll Band, and they still make music together today.

Keith playing guitar with the Rolling Stones, age 19

Keith owns over 350 guitars, but he's never forgotten the very first guitar that his granddad showed him how to play.

Keith playing guitar today

Brian Rasic

Keith, his guitar, and his grandson Orson

Jane Rose

Keith with his fifth grandchild, Otto

Patti Hansen

"The bond, the special bond, between kids and grandparents is unique and should be treasured. This is a story of one of those magical moments. May I be as great a grandfather as Gus was to me."

—Keith Richards

ABOUT THIS BOOK

Creating the art for *Gus & Me* was a labour of love.
When researching the images for this project,

Theodora traveled to England,

consulted family photos,

Keith, age 4

Theodora's rendering

and spoke with her father to draw on his memories.

Keith sketched the "beehive-like" music
shop as inspiration for Theodora.

This book was edited by Megan Tingley and Bethany Strout and designed by Gail Doobinin with art direction by Patti Ann Harris.
The production was supervised by Erika Schwartz, and the production editor was Christine Ma.
The illustrations for this book were done in pen, ink, and collage on paper. The text was set in Bodoni.
Theodora created the hand-lettered display type throughout the interior, except what is on pages 31 and 33, which were created by Keith.
The family photos are included courtesy of the Richards family.

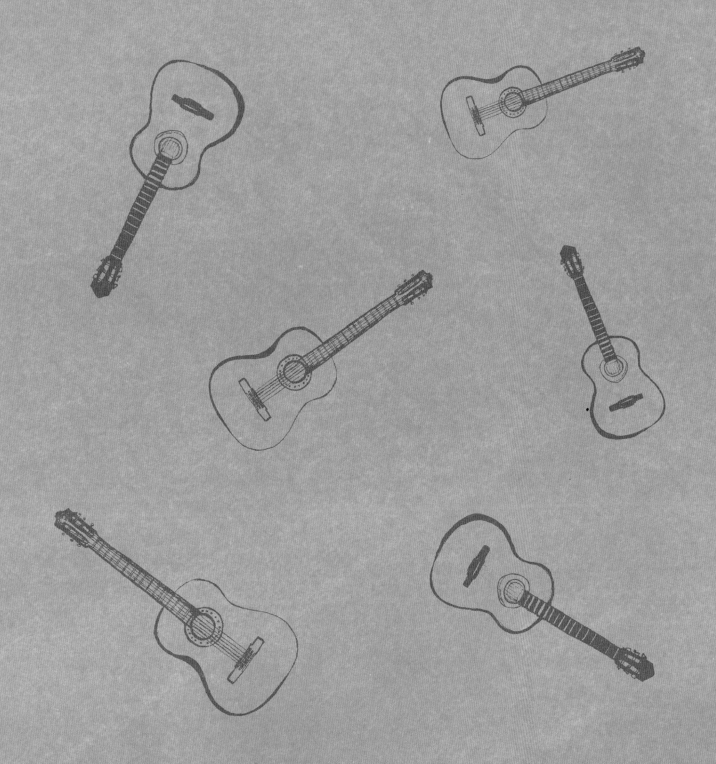

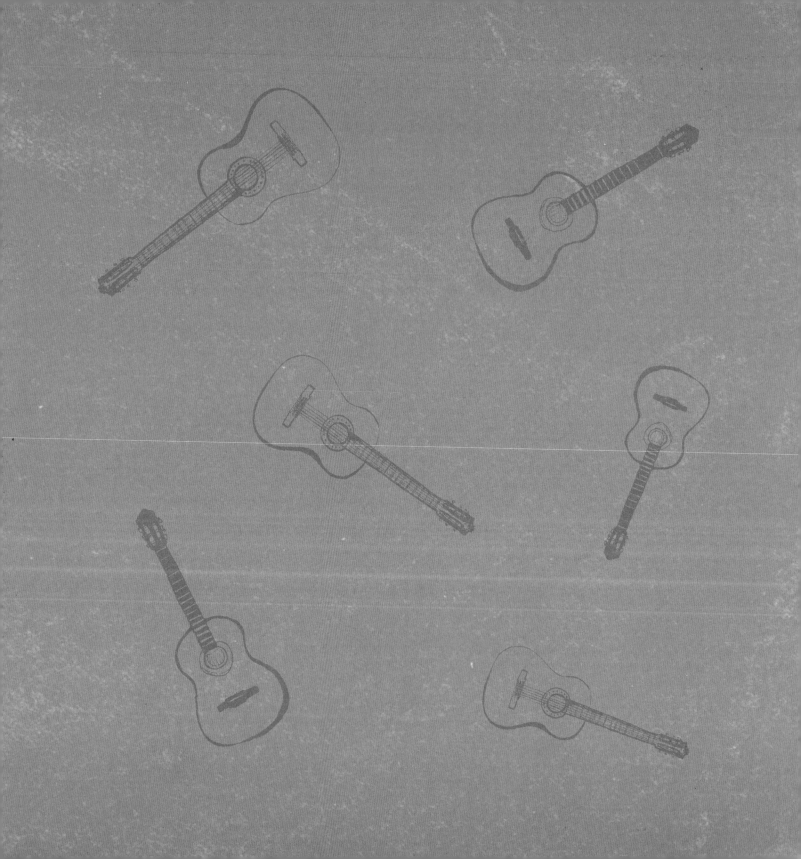